The Toilet is Over-Flowing & The Dog is Wearing My Underwear!

Debbie Roppolo

The Toilet is Over-Flowing &
The Dog is Wearing My Underwear!

Debbie Roppolo

The Toilet is Over-Flowing &
The Dog is Wearing My Underwear!
Debbie Roppolo

DWB PUBLISHING
www.dancingwithbearpublishing.com

The Toilet is Over-Flowing &
The Dog is Wearing My Underwear!

Debbie Roppolo

The Toilet is Over-Flowing &
The Dog is Wearing My Underwear!
Debbie Roppolo

For my dear boys and husband—thank you all for
the love, patience, and laughter through the years.
My dear friend Marie—without you, none of this
would be possible.

The Toilet is Over-Flowing &
The Dog is Wearing My Underwear!
Debbie Roppolo

The Toilet is Over-Flowing &
The Dog is Wearing My Underwear!
Debbie Roppolo

Forward

When I was a child, I entertained my mother with my antics and wild imagination. Okay, I'll be honest—I tortured the poor woman. I had tea parties with chickens where

Purina Chick-Starter™ was the food of choice for all involved. And I married in kindergarten to my (at the time) best guy friend. That lasted all of ten minutes when my grandmother caught us sealing the deal with a kiss in the bushes. I had to give the ring back (made of chewed gum and a pebble) and listen to Mama lecture about why little girls shouldn't kiss boys.

When I was five, I told the ladies at church that Mama gave me cat food as a snack (it was really Cracklin' Oat Bran™), brought a horse into her house ten years later, and a few years after that would ride the same horse across the pasture, no saddle or bridle. It's no wonder why by the time I left home, Mama's once perfect face wore an expression of permanent alarm, her jet-black hair painted with gray streaks. She'd get her revenge by regaling my boyfriends with stories of my adventures.

"Wait and see," she'd say as I laughed. "Parenting isn't as simple as it seems. You're gonna get back what you dish out."

I never understood what she meant or thought for one moment it might be a parents' curse until I had children of my own. Both put me through the parental wringer. As infants, both Jonathan and Joseph waited until we were in public to loudly pass gas. No one ever believed the baby did it.

The Toilet is Over-Flowing &
The Dog is Wearing My Underwear!
Debbie Roppolo

Being a parent has been an educational experience. Thanks to my boys, I've learned that cell phones don't float in water, and a family Dalmatian can be the victim of dot-to-dot sessions, performed with a marker. There have been portraits on crumpled paper, created with my best makeup. And I've had to rescue my underwear off the family dog on more than one occasion, sometimes in front of the company. But because of my precious sons, I've learned to enjoy the simpler things in life—the feel of a loved one's embrace and the beat of their heart as you hold them close, sunsets, and of course, the smell of fresh brewed coffee.

I'm thrilled to share my parenting journey with you, my friends. It's my wish that by reading this, you realize there is always laughter, sometimes mixed with tears, and the human spirit can persevere, no matter how great the odds. Always remember, *La vita e bella! (*Life is beautiful!)

The Toilet is Over-Flowing &
The Dog is Wearing My Underwear!
Debbie Roppolo

~ Chapter One ~
Chasing After Aprons

I'm a TV food show junkie. I find the female cooks
interesting, but if I wanted a quick and nutritious meal in
less than thirty minutes, I'd chip a Lean Cuisine™ out of the
freezer and toss it in the microwave. No, it's the male
chefs who grab my attention.

I can't explain my infatuation. Perhaps it's because
men are wearing aprons, or the way they wield knives like
a circus performer, and the fact they have a direct line to
my soul with food.

My fascination didn't begin recently. It started when
I was five. I remember watching Sesame Street™ one
morning. Cookie Monster appeared on-screen wearing an
apron and chef's hat. Eyes bugging out, I arose from the
floor and walked closer to the television, gaze never
wavering from Cookie Monster's face, a thin river of saliva
trickling down my chin.

"Isn't that cute," my mother whispered to
Daddy.

"Our daughter really wants to learn her letters."

Learn letters my Aunt Fanny. Even at that age, I was
probably envisioning my and Cookie Monster's wedding. Our
registry would be listed at Nabisco™, our house made of
snicker doodles, and he would've never taken off that darn
hat or apron.

My senior year in high school, I dated a young man,
Alec Rotini, who had a lot going for him—looks, a nice
house, and (joy of my heart) a father who was a master

The Toilet is Over-Flowing &
The Dog is Wearing My Underwear!
Debbie Roppolo

chef at a popular restaurant who sometimes appeared on a local morning news show.

Imagine my excitement when after only three months of dating, Alec invited me to Christmas supper. I breezed through the doorway, head held high, acting disinterested as Alec introduced me to his father. Inwardly, I was a melting Christmas gelatin mold.

"I hope you don't mind," Chef Rotini said, tying on an apron, "but making meals together is a family tradition, and we like to involve guests so they can benefit from the experience too."

Mind? Of course I didn't mind. They could have turned into a family of cannibals at that moment, and I would've died a happy person. This was a Christmas I'd never forget.

Like a seasoned ship's captain, Chef Rotini gave out instructions while he cooked. I sat on a stool, watching Alec and his mother slice and dice ingredients. I prayed the chef would forget me. Luck wasn't on my side.

"Can't get away with doing nothing in my kitchen." Chef Rotini hand me a package of ground beef and a slab of bacon. "Here, make patties, and wrap with bacon."

I wished I'd spent more time cooking with Mama. The patty part was self-explanatory, but what about the rest? Shrugging, I waved the slab of pork over my head, and did my best MC Hammer impression.

Silence blanketed the kitchen as the Rolatinis stared, incredulous.

"W-What are you doing, dear?" the chef asked.

"Rapping with the bacon." Tears rolled down my face as Alec erupted into laughter. My insides turned to

The Toilet is Over-Flowing &
The Dog is Wearing My Underwear!
Debbie Roppolo

mush as Chef Rotini wiped away my tears with a corner of his apron.

"Every cook makes mistakes. Think you can handle a salad?" he asked, handing me a head of lettuce.

That seemed safe. I never dreamed my breath mint would fall out of my mouth and play hide-n-seek among the lettuce leaves. Beads of perspiration formed on my lips as I pawed through the salad. Darn. Why did I decide to use a wintergreen Tic-Tac™? My heart leaped into my throat when I heard a voice behind me. "When you toss a salad, you really toss one."

I hoped the person behind me was Mrs. Rotini, that she'd had a sudden onset of male hormones, making her voice deeper. Of course, it was the chef.

"Did you lose something, or do you always throw lettuce all over a counter?" he asked. He took the bowl to the sink and sifted through the greens. "Is this what you're looking for?" he asked, showing me a half-melted breath mint.

In under fifteen minutes, I'd danced with pork, turned his kitchen counter into a demolition area, and tried to poison his family with tainted lettuce. I expected the chef to explode and banish me from his kitchen... and his house forever. Instead, humor lighting his eyes, Chef Rotini rewashed the lettuce, assuring me there was "...no harm done."

Alec and his mother left the kitchen to prepare the dining room. I was alone with the chef. My pulse quickened. I felt myself hyper-ventilating as I watched him, still apron clad, stirring sauce on the stove.

The Toilet is Over-Flowing &
The Dog is Wearing My Underwear!
Debbie Roppolo

"Y-you want me to help Mrs. Rotini?" I asked, wringing my hands.

"No," he said, not taking his eyes off the sauce. "But you can poke my buns to see if they're done."

I jabbed his buns. Unfortunately, he meant the rolls in the oven, not his rear end.

Alec never invited me over again and shortly after that ill-fated holiday dinner, he ended our relationship. My fascination with cooks and chefs has plagued me most of my life. So, isn't it logical that I married a man who's highly skilled in the kitchen? Some women like men in uniforms. I chase after men who wear aprons.

~ Chapter Two ~
All I Asked for Was A Dog

Children morph into strange, aloof creatures the minute they enter their teen years. Baby dolls and toy trucks are tossed aside, and love affairs with mirrors form. Blue-haired performers screeching about funky chickens and sexy tractors replace dancing dinosaurs crooning tinkly tunes about circles and colors. Yes, these blossoming young people know what they want in life and resent adults who try to persuade them otherwise.

I was no exception. Before the candle wax hardened on my thirteenth birthday cake, I believed my parents were dumber than soap and were two days, maximum, away from taking Geritol™ and living in a retirement home. I also had my life-plan formulated. It didn't matter the sight of a scab made me woozy; I planned to be a veterinarian, drive a Maserati, and own a horse racing stable.

Parenting was never an option.

Mama thought differently. "Embrace motherhood," she said, "it's your destiny; it's so rewarding."

I disagreed. I didn't believe sleep deprivation and wearing a permanent badge of spit-up made me a candidate for a Nobel Peace Prize. And I never saw game show contestants elated over a years' supply of dirty diapers. Instead, I would raise a puppy. Dogs didn't need burped after every meal (just try throwing a Doberman over your shoulder) or dressed in fancy clothes. As a canine owner, I wouldn't have to wash strained peas from my hair,

13

The Toilet is Over-Flowing &
The Dog is Wearing My Underwear!
Debbie Roppolo

worry about breast vs. bottle feeding, or ask grocery store
stockers what hemorrhoid cream they recommended.

I believed children were just noisy small people,
getting their way by throwing fits in public. I tried that
once when a club denied me access. The only thing I gained
was dirty clothes and a brief stint in the back of a patrol
car. The next day, the responding officer, John, called. We
began dating, and a year later, married. Evidently the sight
of a well-groomed twenty-one-year-old rolling in the dirt
screaming piqued his interest.

Most couples go through a honeymoon phase, and
short of molding my footprints in cement, John treated me
like a princess. But I was melancholy, there was something
missing in my life. My childhood dreams of being a vet
disappeared, but I vowed to fulfill my goal of owning a dog,
believing that would fill the void.

Husbands rid bathrooms of giant, mutant spiders win
wrestling matches with stubborn jar lids, and double as
furniture for toddlers. But they're also cursed with the
ability to hear select words and translate the meaning to
their own liking. That became obvious when I told John of
my emptiness and need for canine companionship. Three
months later, I was pregnant and still dogless.

I wish I'd radiated beauty like other pregnant
women. My hair resembled limp spaghetti. I had dark
circles under my eyes a raccoon would be envious of, and
there was no doubt roadkill could beat me in a beauty
contest.

Once, feeling nauseous, I waited outside a store,
leaning against the wall, sipping 7-Up™ while John finished
the shopping. Without a word, a well-dressed, elderly

The Toilet is Over-Flowing &
The Dog is Wearing My Underwear!
Debbie Roppolo

woman dropped several coins into my cup. "I hope they find a cure for your illness soon."

"They will, in about six months," I replied glibly.

Tears glistened in the woman's eyes. "What hope. Such an unbeatable spirit," she whispered, scurrying away.

Finally, the day arrived when our son, Jonathan, was born. Arm wavering like an overcooked noodle, he reached out a tiny hand, touching my cheek and my heart. Blinking back tears, I stared at the bundle in my arms. He looked like ET's cousin, but I adored him. Kids weren't so bad after all.

Eight years later, I again felt empty. Once more, I asked John for a puppy. Nine months later, I had my second son, Joseph.

As a preschooler, some of Joseph's greatest joys were chasing cars and trying to eat kibble spilled on supermarket floors. At least that time I got a little closer to getting what I asked for.

~ Chapter Three ~
June and the Gang Would Be Proud

As an adolescent, I believed parenting would be a breeze. If I had known motherhood entailed fishing cell phones from toilets and pulling cocoa puffs out of noses, I'd have become a nun. I would've evicted baby chicks from my playhouse, swaddled dolls, and listened to every conversation about hemorrhoids, infant bowel movements, and coupons my mother's quilting group had.

Instead, television characters were my role models. I watched soap opera starlets tell their lovers they were pregnant. In the next episode, these same women carried the baby for nine months, obliterated drug cartels, and gave birth, all with hair and makeup intact. And June Cleaver could plan a school fundraiser, knit a sweater, solve the Beaver's problems, and have dinner for Ward all in less than thirty minutes. Being a parent was simple. Reality bit a few days after I had my first child, Jonathan.

"Just change the diaper, then you're set to go home," Nurse Gertrude said, handing me the baby.

I struggled to take a deep breath. This was a test I'd fail. I imagined, years later, Jonathan appearing on talk shows, saying I'd had the parenting instincts of a kumquat, and I wrecked his life. And I can't blame him. I didn't prepare for this new chapter in my life.
I hadn't bothered reading many books. None of the authors could explain my bladder's love affair with gas stations, or why my ankles morphed into cantaloupes.

The Toilet is Over-Flowing &
The Dog is Wearing My Underwear!
Debbie Roppolo

Parenting classes were a waste too. I already knew how to breathe. The teacher lost credibility when she had us place clothespins on our earlobes, simulating labor. My mother always told me, "Babies come from you know where." The last time I'd checked, the ear canals weren't "you know where."

Now I stared at the patterns in the floor, searching my brain for knowledge I'd gained over the last few months. "How about storage bags?" I suggested. "Everything stays fresher with Ziploc™. We could cut leg holes..."

My confidence waned as Nurse Gertrude stared at me, incredulous. She was a no-nonsense woman, having little patience with inept parents, and judging from her deepening scowl, a cannibalistic hamster would beat me out for Mother-Of-The-Year.

I thought that was the last paternal hurdle I'd overcome. Again, I was wrong.

The next several months were an educative experience. Jonathan learned to time his outbursts the minute my head touched a pillow. I discovered the meaning of sleep deprivation.

I diapered cakes and frosted the baby. Car keys hid behind bags of peas in the freezer, and I tried to start the car with fish sticks. Shopping, something I'd excelled at in the past, became harder than stealing cocoa from a chocoholic. I'd peruse grocery store aisles, thumping bald produce men in the head to check for ripeness, and tried taking naps in the bakery.

Managing a household and raising a child wasn't any easier. Once, I shoved a pacifier in the fee-collecting

The Toilet is Over-Flowing &
The Dog is Wearing My Underwear!
Debbie Roppolo

paperboy's mouth and handed Jonathan a twenty-dollar
bill. We never received another newspaper, and it's no
wonder my now teenaged son expects money every time he
cries. I believe my parenting skills have improved over the
years. I can fix a drain, cook a roast, and unstop a toilet,
all while helping with algebra homework. The other day, I
disrupted a band of cookie-selling girl scouts and
confiscated their supply. June and the soap opera moms
would be proud.

The Toilet is Over-Flowing &
The Dog is Wearing My Underwear!
Debbie Roppolo

~ Chapter Four ~
Journey from Sanity

During the late spring and early summer, certain things remain constant—heat indexes can be measured by the amount of drool on a dog's tongue, and vinyl auto interior isn't kind to bare legs—especially mine.

Vacation from school begins, and around breakfast tables nation-wide, summer plans are debated. Some families celebrate by buying new beachwear and embarking on trips. Not mine.

It's in the best interest of humanity I wear nothing shorter than a granny-type nightgown. My thighs meet more than the U.N. peace talks. My rump hangs past my ankles and waves goodbye long after I've left the company of others. Once, I tried on a purple swimsuit at a local department store. I looked like a violet version of the Pillsbury Doughboy™, and a young man paid me twenty bucks to put my clothes back on.

The minute my family takes a vacation, Chaos becomes the house sitter. Dirty towels will backstroke in overflowing toilet water. Stray dogs will break-dance and play poker in my flowerbed. Long forgotten leftovers, wearing a full coat of fur, will venture out of the fridge and form their own civilization.

Instead, we have recreation at home. Why hike up a scenic hill when one can chase the lingerie-wearing family dog down the street? Booking an expensive fishing trip

The Toilet is Over-Flowing &
The Dog is Wearing My Underwear!
Debbie Roppolo

isn't necessary. We achieve the same thrill by rescuing the TV remote from the toilet.

One morning though, my husband, John, took a sip of coffee, and asked: "Wanna go on a trip?"

It stunned me to hear intelligible words. John and I aren't morning people, conversing through eye rolls and grunts until the first pot of coffee is downed. We never realized how bad our break-down in morning communication was until our youngest son took us to kindergarten and tried to pass us off at Show-and-Tell as the only living cave people.

"Are you talking to the Mrs. Butterworth™ bottle again?" I asked. "She's not real, that's just a commercial." My husband snorted. "I only talked to her one time to entertain the kids. So, wanna go to the beach or not?"
He had to be kidding. I would give the cat a manicure if it meant getting away from dishes that refused to wash themselves, and phone solicitors who inquired about my health but didn't want to hear about my bunion.
The next morning, our adventure began. There are children who are a pleasure to travel with. Clothes unstained, fingers booger-free, they open the door for their parents, say "please" and "thank-you," and barely speak above a whisper. My two boys fought over earphones, declared they were weak with hunger, and created a mural with spit on the rear window, all before we left the driveway.

Three hours, a dozen fights over a half-melted Tic-tac™ stuck to the floorboard, we stopped in a small town to eat. The restaurant was a mom-and-pop place, the walls covered in tattered pictures and yellowing newspaper clippings of local heroes. I followed my husband and children through the eatery, seething inwardly as several

The Toilet is Over-Flowing &
The Dog is Wearing My Underwear!
Debbie Roppolo

pairs of eyes ogled us. *Good grief, hadn't they seen a tourist before?*

As I was taking my seat, a waiter whispered in my ear, "Madam, I believe you have a problem."

Eyes blazing, forcing a smile, I turned and said, "For the past several hours, I've worn a permanent wig of spitballs and endured foot odor bad enough to choke a buzzard. And at the last gas station, I almost had to pledge marriage to get the restroom key from the attendant."

I gritted my teeth and continued. "And now you people treat me like I'm zombie roadkill. So yes, I have a problem. I—"

Fidgeting with his tie, the waiter cleared his throat, leaned closer, and whispered, "That's a great speech madam, and I sympathize with your plight, but I'd take you more seriously if you un-tucked the back of your dress from your pantyhose."

The Toilet is Over-Flowing &
The Dog is Wearing My Underwear!
Debbie Roppolo

~ Chapter Five ~
Marks on the Heart

"Your son, Joseph, has autism."

I dug my fingernails into the arm of the chair, feeling that at any moment I'd sink into the floor. That wasn't the diagnosis I'd expected to hear from the doctor.

A short time after his third birthday, Joseph's speech progression slowed. My husband and I were both concerned, though not overly alarmed. Our older son, Jonathan, had a speech delay at this age. Joseph would have speech therapy, empowering him to overcome this obstacle, just as his brother had. But autism? I shook my head.

The doctor was wrong.

Across the room, Joseph rummaged through a toy box. He giggled as he pulled a plastic phone from the heap. I suppressed my laughter. As usual, my son's joy was infectious. He was so happy; all the autistic children I had ever seen were withdrawn. There was no way Joseph was autistic.

"That can't be right," I insisted. "Look at him. He's happy. He can read words too advanced for his age." A lump formed in my throat as Joseph, smiling, climbed into my lap and wrapped his arms around my neck. Tears ran down my face as I felt his breath on my cheek, his heart pounding against my chest. In my eyes, my child was perfect. Now a total stranger was telling me he wasn't. "And video games. He can buy games on my cell phone," I sobbed.

The Toilet is Over-Flowing &
The Dog is Wearing My Underwear!
Debbie Roppolo

The doctor cleared her throat and said, "Joseph is what we call 'high-functioning autistic'. That means he's of average intelligence or above. But," she continued, "make no excuses. Treat him like you would a typical child, or you'll let autism cripple him. Do you under- stand?"

The only thing I understood is that I had plans for Joseph. He'd be a leader, leaving his mark on every life he touched. Now those goals were slipping away, faster than water through a sieve.

In the following weeks, I floundered in a well of depression. I doubted my ability as a parent. I berated myself, believing I would've noticed the symptoms earlier if I'd have spent more time with Joseph and less on my writing.

And it didn't boost my self-esteem when people said, "My goodness, what did you do while you were pregnant?" or "I guess it's genetic. From your side of the family?" No matter what I said, they made it obvious I was the one to blame for Joseph's condition.

I hated going out in public. It was then Joseph acted the most autistic. He yelled spontaneously, rocked back and forth, and slapped his face. All of which drew stares and whispers from onlookers. I hated them all, especially the ones with well-behaved, typical children. And I detested myself for not wanting to be seen with my precious son.

To de-stress and maintain my sanity, I took nightly walks. One night, as I had so many times in the past, I looked to the heavens for answers to sooth my troubled heart. As I gazed at the stars, twinkling like gems against a canvas of black velvet, I came upon a realization. It wasn't

The Toilet is Over-Flowing &
The Dog is Wearing My Underwear!
Debbie Roppolo

my fault. I didn't cause Joseph to be autistic. I couldn't have done anything to prevent it. I could only move forward and do what I could to help my son overcome his disorder.

I stopped placing blame on my husband, and began working with him, researching different programs and placing Joseph in occupational and speech therapy. I read everything I could, educating myself and other people on the disorder.

Though it was difficult, I saw Joseph as he really was, a perpetual, mischievous ball of energy, not much different from other children his age. I marveled over how he lived every second to its fullest, not caring what people thought.

Once, in the grocery store, he burst into gleeful, spontaneous yells. Cringing as passersby gave us icy stares, I tried in vain to silence him. "Oh, let him holler," an elderly woman said, breaking into a toothless grin. "He's just making a joyful noise, that's all. Warms my heart to hear him."

Joseph pondered things I took for granted—the way a raindrop left a crooked path on the window, the *swoosh* of wings as birds took flight. Even the setting of the sun left him in breathless wonder. Following his lead, I too marveled at the little things in life, and I couldn't believe what I'd been missing.

As it was, Joseph hadn't strayed too far away from my goals. He was leaving his mark on every life he touched—especially mine.

~ Chapter Six ~
As the Coffee Bean Turns

Throughout the world there are women who paint their cat's toenails, re-tile the kitchen counter, and fix a three-course breakfast for their family, all before the rooster crows and with a smile on their face.

My mother was that type of lady. Stepford wife-like cheerful, she helped with last-minute homework quandaries while making my dad's lunch. I didn't learn until years later that the minute my bus was out of sight, she collapsed in the bed and slept a couple of more hours.

I can't even pretend to be a morning person. Speaking takes too much effort. Slow dancing with a hot toaster would be less painful than engaging in cheerful breakfast conversation. I masquerade flattened cupcakes as gourmet flapjacks, make phone solicitors cry, and refer to my children using pronouns instead of their names. It's no secret either, that without caffeine, I have the intelligence of a paper clip. In the past, I've poured Tabasco™ sauce in my juice glass, had a detailed conversation with a fence post, believing it was my husband John, and gone to the supermarket wearing my bra on the outside of my clothes.

One morning, after years of pampering and hero worship, Mr. Coffee™ ended our affair. There was no warning, no sign he was unhappy with our relationship. He sat silently on the counter, mocking me with an empty carafe.

25

The Toilet is Over-Flowing &
The Dog is Wearing My Underwear!
Debbie Roppolo

My head reeling from lack of caffeine, I took the dog to the veterinarian, my teenager, Jonathan, to high school, and dropped my son, Joseph, off at pre-school. Ten minutes after arriving home, the vet's office called.

"Mrs. Roppolo, you had an appointment to have your dog spade," the receptionist said.

I cringed and tugged at the phone cord. Her chipper voice grated like squeaky chalk on a blackboard. Taking a deep breath, I struggled to be polite. "Do what you have to do, worm it, clip its nails, and operate."

There was silence, followed by hysterical laughter. "You... you... don't understand," the woman said, trying to regain her composure. "That would be simple to do, but you left your son here instead of the dog."

As a toddler, Jonathan stole kibble from the dog's bowl, chased the ice cream man down the street, and tried drinking water from the toilet. Now his hair hung past his eyes, making him the envy of sheepdogs. Given those circumstances, anyone would have made my mistake. Later that same day, John and I discussed my mother's stay with us after her heart surgery. Jonathan, still angry over his trip to the vet, huddled over a parenting magazine, reading aloud tips about transporting children. After the plans about Mom were completed, we talked about the dog's surgery and aftercare when she returned home. "We'll need to put a collar on her and tie her up," I told John.

My husband frowned and shook his head. "She's just going to holler and wake the neighbors. Let's put her in the garage."

The Toilet is Over-Flowing &
The Dog is Wearing My Underwear!
Debbie Roppolo

"What if she makes a mess? You know how she loves magazines, and there are three stacks of them in that back corner."

John sipped his coffee. "Easy, we just whack her with a newspaper. And speaking of messes..." he continued, wagging his finger at me, "if she has an accident in the garage, we'll have to rub her nose in it."

I shook my head. "I can't do that, it's too cruel."

"Have it your way, she's your responsibility."

Jonathan pushed his chair back, aghast. "You are the cruelest people I've ever known. How could you put my grandmother in the garage? Granny and I might be in your way sometimes, but we don't deserve to be treated like dogs. How dare you!"

Silence blanketed the room. In his effort to make it clear I wasn't mother-of-the-year material, Jonathan had missed the transition in conversations.

His father and I erupted in laughter.

"Don't see what's so funny," my son pouted. "What's next, feeding Joseph a bowl of Meow Mix™ at breakfast?"

"Son," John said, wiping his eyes. "We're talking about the dog, not Granny.

Jonathan stomped to the door, surrounded by the sound by his father's and my laughter. "It's not my fault," he grumbled. "I didn't have my cocoa this morning, and I haven't been able to function right all day."

Alas, caffeine has claimed another generation of my family.

The Toilet is Over-Flowing &
The Dog is Wearing My Underwear!
Debbie Roppolo

~ Chapter Seven ~
If the Pot Breaks, My Sanity will Fall...

I looked at my alarm clock and groaned—five o'clock.

Normally at that hour I'd be dreaming of towels that threw themselves in the hamper and self-cleaning, dancing toilets. But the night before, bitten by the maternal bug, I volunteered to accompany my husband, John, and our sons, Jonathan and Joseph, to a rabbit show several hours away. Now, as I stumbled down the hallway, I thought that either my cheese had slipped off its cracker or I was very devoted to my children.

I paused in the kitchen doorway, horrified at what I saw. The Mr. Coffee™ sat on the counter, java dribbling from a crack in its pot onto the floor. Amber-colored cat tracks decorated the linoleum, leading to a puddle of coffee-scented feline puke under the kitchen table.

Great. In just under an hour, we'd be leaving. I'd have just enough time to clean the mess, make breakfast, and get dressed. There'd be no coffee for me that morning unless I planned to lick it off the floor—at that point, I was considering it.

I have made early-calling phone solicitors cry and the paperboy flee in terror. The last time I awoke this early, I poured dish detergent in my coffee and caught myself putting my youngest son outside and dressing the cat for school.

If my family had any hopes of a halfway pleasant trip, I had to have caffeine... now.

The Toilet is Over-Flowing &
The Dog is Wearing My Underwear!
Debbie Roppolo

I put a spare pot in the Mr. Coffee™, pleading with the caffeine gods to hurry the ancient machine. Forty-five minutes later it wheezed to a stop, finishing just in time for my husband, John, to empty the pot into his travel mug.

"Oh, I'm sorry. Did you want any of this?"

Jerk. He had to be kidding. I would've sold my children for the opportunity to just suck on one tiny coffee ground. Still, I had my pride. I wouldn't give him the pleasure of seeing me beg.

"I'll be fine," I said, folding my arms.

John shrugged. "Suit yourself then. Sure is good," he said, smacking his lips.

I gritted my teeth. If he was smart, he'd run away. He does not know how close his mustache and my Epilady™ were to having a date.

I stumbled out the door and slithered into the front seat of the car. John and the boys piled in, chattering excitedly. I huddled against the passenger window and had my pity-party. They don't care I'm an aching, caffeine-deprived pile of gelatin. No, as far as they're concerned, I'm part of the car, nothing more than bug guts on the windshield.

Three hours, one potty break, and forty-five billboards for truck stops (believe me, I counted) later, we arrived at the show. We parked beneath an aging oak tree, bedecked in a dress of Spanish moss.

In a child's opinion, anyone over the age of twenty-five has one foot on Medicare and the other in the grave. Jonathan insisted I relax while he and the other "men" of the family registered our rabbits. He pointed to an elderly

The Toilet is Over-Flowing &
The Dog is Wearing My Underwear!
Debbie Roppolo

woman sitting at a nearby picnic table. "There's someone your age to talk to. Can you make it over there? Do you need my help, maybe a stick to walk with?" he shouted in my ear.

I frowned and shook my head. One shimmer of gray in my hair waved hello to the world the week before, and now my son was contemplating brochures for rest homes. The same child who, just days before, begged me to slow down and let him take a break after a half-mile trek around the hospital's walking trail.

"I'll see if I can make it without breaking a hip," I snarled, walking toward the table. As I sat, the older woman grabbed my arm.

"There's an ass," she said, pointing at my bottom. I forced a smile, struggling to be polite. I'd already dealt with no coffee, my son treating me like a Geritol™ candidate, and now this woman was talking about my rump.

"Yes, it is," I replied, trying to take my seat.

"Don't tell me you're gonna sit on it," she said, her dried apple face a picture of disbelief.

I've always respected my elders, but this lady's infatuation with my backside was becoming more than I could handle.

"Well, yes. Isn't your ass what you sit on?"

"Not ass, you ninny. Asp, ASP!" she yelled, pointing with her cane to a spiny, dangerous-looking worm on the bench just beneath me. Had I sat on it, I would have received a nasty sting.

My face turned crimson with embarrassment. "I'm sorry... I-I didn't have my coffee this morning and—"

The Toilet is Over-Flowing &
The Dog is Wearing My Underwear!
Debbie Roppolo

"Coffee, my Aunt Fanny," the woman barked. "It's those darn things you young people plug in your ears to listen to music. Piepods or something like that. Damages your hearing."

Rising to her feet, she tottered away, leaving me to realize I was a coffee dependent fool who suffered from acute foot-in-the-mouth disease. What else is new?

~ Chapter Eight ~
Put Your Best Face Forward

I leaned against the doorway, fighting sleep and hoping to make sense of the scene unfolding in front of me. Part of me wished it was dream—I was really relaxing on a beach in Cancun, instead of my bunny slippers doing the backstroke in toilet water.

Still, the mom in me wanted to know why, when most mornings it'd take a backhoe to get him out of bed, my four-year-old was standing in the middle of the bathroom, plunger in hand. A steady stream of water overflowed the toilet behind him.

"I told you it was bad," my thirteen-year-old, Jonathan, said. He cleared his throat. "It **was** a lot worse, but I cleaned it up a bit."

I opened an eye and groaned. Towels lay in the mess resembling soggy islands. And judging from the empty bin, he'd used every towel in the linen closet. *Great, more laundry to do. Just the way I wanted to spend a summer morning.* I reasoned Jonathan had taken the initiative.

This, coming from a soul who would spill and leave the spot alone until it was almost strong enough to clean up itself.

He was taking steps toward adulthood

Joseph backed against the tub, looking like a frightened fawn. I took a deep breath, struggling to find patience. My baby was diagnosed with autism two years earlier, making communication difficult, if not impossible. I spoke slowly and clearly. "What happened, Joe?"

The Toilet is Over-Flowing &
The Dog is Wearing My Underwear!
Debbie Roppolo

My younger son burst into tears. "What happened, Joe?" he repeated between sobs.

"Maybe he was pretending he was King Neptune. We watched *The Little Mermaid* yesterday," Jonathan offered.

I stepped between the two boys before Joseph knighted his brother with the toilet plunger.

Walking around the house, and through the process of elimination, Jonathan and I pieced the story together. The Beta fish, George, though he had survived much longer (five months) than any of his predecessors, had gone to his fishy reward. Joseph had discovered the loss, and wanting to pay tribute, gave him a burial in the closest thing to the sea, and in my blush brush box.

An hour and many promises of Pop Tarts™, a visit to the pet store for an unsuspecting George II for Joseph, and I finished cleaning the mess in our bathroom.

I moaned as I stood. It was funny how time changed the human body. In my twenties I could ride my horse all day, dance the night away, and take a hike the next morning, all with little to no sleep. Now I thought myself a party animal if I stayed awake past ten at night, and my back did a perfect Rice Krispies™ impersonation (snap, crackle and pop) when I rolled out of bed every morning.

I'd spent many hours during my childhood, watching my mother as she applied cold creams and toners to her skin every night.

"After all precious," she said, "a lady must always put her best face forward."

That morning, my mother would've been horrified at the sight of my reflection in the mirror. I could have checked the bags beneath my eyes at a baggage claim, and

The Toilet is Over-Flowing &
The Dog is Wearing My Underwear!
Debbie Roppolo

the dark circles highlighting them would have made a raccoon envious.

Pampering wasn't something I engaged in, not for myself, but I needed to escape the zombie look my face currently sported. Stress seeped from my body as I smeared on the hot-pink facial mask, enjoying the coolness of the clay enveloping my skin.

A knock at the door interrupted my relaxation. A truck with the words *SMITH'S DEVELOPING* emblazoned on the side sat in my drive. Standing on my porch was a young man, petting my dog, Blue. Huskies are notorious for being poor watch dogs, but as I watched the guy scratch Blue's stomach, there was no doubt, if scratched in the proper place, my dog would help a burglar carry our valuables out of the house.

Traitorous dog.

A plan formed when I scratched my nose. Sometimes the need to be mischievous and snarky overwhelms all reason, and I go with the flow.

The man startled as I opened the door and eyed my face suspiciously. "I umm… just wanted to know who owns that acreage beside you." He shifted uncomfortably. "But I can come back when you're not busy."

I shrugged. "Just decorating a cake. I really get into my work. Wanna piece?"

"I see. Hmm… no… unnecessary… but thanks." The young man almost fell over Blue, still laying on the porch, in his haste to leave.

Mama was wrong. Sometimes it pays not to put your best face forward.

The Toilet is Over-Flowing &
The Dog is Wearing My Underwear!
Debbie Roppolo

~ Chapter Nine ~
Adventures in the Aisles

I investigated my pantry and groaned. "Mother Hubbard has nothing on me." Abandoned half-eaten snacks played peek-a-boo behind dust bunnies on the top shelf. Jars of pickles (victims of last summer's canning efforts, now science experiments) huddled together in a dark corner. It was enough to make any self-respecting field mouse pack up its things and leave. Unless I smashed a couple of stale Hostess™ cupcakes flat and tried to pass them off as gourmet pancakes at Christmas dinner, I'd have to go to the store.

Some people enjoy trips to the supermarket. They rejoice over great deals and engage in gossip rank enough to curdle milk in the dairy case.

I would rather have a root canal performed by a rookie dental student. Let's face it—the reduced price of bladder pads and beans doesn't excite me. I don't enjoy waltzing down aisles to the Muzak™ version of "Like a Virgin," with elderly men. And unless it bears a striking resemblance to a known celebrity, I don't want to hear what Joan Q's son's bowel movement looked like.

I do well to withstand an hour of wrestling with produce bags, dodging kids on runaway scooters, and cereal dropped on my head before succumbing to the urge of hijacking a Hershey's™ truck and devouring its entire cargo. Yes, a jaunt to the grocery store means someone is going to get hurt, and usually it's me.

The Toilet is Over-Flowing &
The Dog is Wearing My Underwear!
Debbie Roppolo

In previous shopping gigs, people in motorized shopping carts have flattened me. And during my last trip, I wrestled with an elderly woman over a marked-down pot roast. "Let go before I put a bobby pin where only your proctologist can find it," the feisty senior threatened. Yanking the meat out of my hands, she swaggered away, victorious.

The only thing I'd won was a trip into the freezer trough, a face-full of ground chuck, and the seat of my pants ripped, exposing my polka-dot panties. I'd left the store that day with both my body and ego bruised.

My boys, Jonathan and Joseph, boycott "grocery shopping with Mom" unless I agree to sign a waiver guaranteeing *Search & Rescue* will be on standby. Could it be because I once ran Joseph and the racecar-shaped cart into a display of toilet paper? For days afterward, potty training was at a standstill. Every time Joseph saw a roll of two-ply, he'd break into a sweat and run out of the bathroom, believing the "bad potty paper" would attack him.

Or perhaps it's because another time I'd driven away from the store, leaving Jonathan and a gallon of ice cream on the sidewalk.

However, this time would be different. I breezed through the doors of the store, children in tow, determined to have a normal shopping trip.

"Mama isn't gonna show you her underwear today," Joseph told the door greeter. "She doesn't wanna make the meat spoil."

"He doesn't know what he's saying," Jonathan interjected. "Mama dropped him on his head too many times when he was a baby."

The Toilet is Over-Flowing &
The Dog is Wearing My Underwear!
Debbie Roppolo

I gritted my teeth and walked away, fighting the urge to drop my children in the "no deposit, no return" bin.

With the skill of a racecar driver, I manipulated the shopping cart through empty boxes left in the middle of aisles, and confused Christmas shoppers. Like a boxer, I ducked and wove as children threw cereal boxes past my head toward their mothers' cart. By aisle six, I was giddy with excitement. At last, I was having a normal shopping experience.

"Let's grab the honey, then we'll be ready to go," I told the kids.

We perused the aisles but could not find the golden liquid. Just as we were giving up, we saw her...the elusive stocker. Stockers are solitary, shy creatures, bolting at the sight of customers, sometimes becoming vicious when cornered and asked questions beginning with "Where is..." and "Do you know...?"

I approached the stock woman, careful not to alarm her.

"Where is..."

The woman turned, eyes blazing, hands twisting a bag of potato flakes she held in her grasp.

I gulped and rephrased my sentence. "I mean... could you please point me to the direction of the honey?"

The stocker smiled. It was obvious I was a seasoned, well-trained shopper.

My jaw dropped as I watched the woman scratch her bottom with the bag of potatoes she'd been holding. I closed my eyes, praying that for once in his young, opinionated life, my teenager wouldn't say a word.

The Toilet is Over-Flowing &
The Dog is Wearing My Underwear!
Debbie Roppolo

The harder the stocker thought, the further she pushed the potatoes into her butt crack. My stomach heaved when she placed the same bag of potatoes on the shelf with the others.

"I really don't know where it is," she said. "I don't work in this department—usually the deli."

My stomach tap-dancing, I forwent the honey, and indulge in a Maalox™ smoothie once I got home. "Maybe she's working on a new concept of scratch-n-sniff packaging," Jonathan whispered as we headed to the register. Shopping. In my family, it isn't just an errand, it's an adventure.

~ Chapter Ten ~
I'll Trade You a Snoopy Lunch Bag for Some Sex Appeal

On his first day as a high school freshman, my son, Jonathan, left home carrying a Snoopy™ lunch bag. He returned that afternoon with sex appeal.

He was giddy as he told of girls asking for his name and phone number. He glowed (I was nauseated) as he spoke of one girl in particular, Vixen. She'd pinched his cheeks and said he was cute.

"You'll love her, Mom. She's just like you," my son said.

I doubted that. No teenaged girl I knew of fussed about lime build-up in toilets or complained about bunions to sack boys at the local grocery store.

"Anyway," Jonathan continued, "she's coming home with me after school tomorrow."

Great. Most kids carry home schoolwork or papers to be signed—my son brings home girls. Wasn't it just yesterday Jonathan was shoving orange seeds up his nose and finger-painting the cat? Wasn't he just out of diapers?

Jonathan took meat, cheese, and pickles out of the fridge and sat them by his books. I sighed as I watched my Cupid-struck child smear mayo on his math book and attempt to open the bread bag to page ten.

The Toilet is Over-Flowing &
The Dog is Wearing My Underwear!
Debbie Roppolo

"I'd like to give Vixen a present tomorrow. What do you suggest?"

"How about a nice chastity belt?" I mumbled. Any gal who pinched my baby's cheeks (I didn't want to know which cheeks) and had the name of "Vixen" was trouble.

Jonathan sighed and shook his head. "Mom, please. Just give the girl a chance. Besides," he pointed out, "you always say 'never judge a book by its covers.'"

I stabbed my fingernail into an orange and took my irritation out on its peel. Great. Out of all the lectures I'd given him over the years, he had to listen to that one. I hoped Vixen wasn't a book written in Braille.

"All I'm saying," I countered, "is that you need to be careful. I don't wanna be a grandma before I'm forty." I doubted he heard me. In his opinion, I'm a tottering old fool who isn't intelligent enough to cross the street by herself.

The next afternoon, I met the girl who was my supposed double. Evidently, Jonathan thought I engaged in activities more risqué than foraging for lost socks in the washer.

Attired in hip-hugger shorts and a wrinkled peek-a-boo shirt, Vixen looked fresh off the street corner. Nausea and chills enveloped my body. I was certain that Mrs. Hinkley had seen Vixen walk into the house. The neighborhood joke was that with Mrs. Hinkley living in the area, there was no need for newspapers. From recent affairs to who had hemorrhoids, she kept the block informed.

A few mornings ago, the plumber stopped by to refund money I'd overpaid him for a previous repair. As he drove away, I glimpsed my senior snooper peeping from

The Toilet is Over-Flowing &
The Dog is Wearing My Underwear!
Debbie Roppolo

behind her living room curtains. Thinking I'd give her something to gossip about other than my loaves of bread not even the birds would eat, I waved at her and shouted, "Isn't he a dream?" I'd joked. "He's a regular and tips well."

Now I wondered if my joking had been a good idea. No doubt she was breaking fingernails in her haste to dial the police department. I imagined the note I'd leave for my husband, John.

> *Sorry honey, but dinner won't*
> *be served for the next five to ten years.*
> Be a dear, bring bail money to the
> police department *would you? I've been*
> *arrested for running a house of*
> *prostitution.*
>
> *Love ya! Deb*

My heart pounding, I threw open the door, looking behind the shrubs and up and down the street.

"Looking for something?" Jonathan whispered.

"The vice squad."

"Relax," he grumbled.

Easy for him to say. He wouldn't be the one arrested and have a cellmate by the name of Big Bertha who didn't believe in personal hygiene.

I took a deep breath and regained my composure. What if Jonathan was right? Perhaps beneath Vixen's rough cover lurked the intelligence of a master scholar.

The Toilet is Over-Flowing &
The Dog is Wearing My Underwear!
Debbie Roppolo

Managing a shaky smile, I walked over to her and held out my hand. "Nice to meet you. I'm—"

My stomach heaved when Vixen took a wad of gum out of her mouth and stuck it behind her ear. "I know who you be, chick," she replied, pumping my hand. "Hope ya don't mind. We're gonna study Astrology up in Jonathan's room."

"Astronomy," my son corrected.

Vixen sniffed. "Whatever. They both involve stars, right?"

Scholar she wasn't. In fact, she was the girl who'd make even June Cleaver reach for a bottle of gin. As Vixen led Jonathan up the stairs, I envisioned their children and family gatherings. The grandchildren would each sport wads of gum (bigger than platters) behind their ears and call me "Chick" instead of "Grandma."

Beef jerky and beer nuts would replace roast turkey and mashed potatoes on the holiday table. Russian Beer Roulette would supplant singing carols around the piano.

I couldn't let any of that happen. "You can study in the living room," I insisted. "The light is better here, and dinner will be ready soon."

Vixen regarded me before prancing down the stairs. "Whateva floats ya boat, honey," she said, giggling as my son pulled her onto the couch beside him.

Woebegone, I stood at the kitchen sink, scraping carrots into nothingness. I glanced at the young couple in the living room. My heart sank as I watched Jonathan put his arm around Vixen while she snuggled against his shoulder.

Suddenly, the girl leaped off the couch. "I-I gotta go home," she mumbled.

The Toilet is Over-Flowing &
The Dog is Wearing My Underwear!
Debbie Roppolo

I could barely suppress my joy as Vixen ran out the front door. But my happiness dissolved as I watched a dejected Jonathan shuffle towards the stairs. "What happened to Vixen?"

Jonathan shook his head. "Well, she tried to kiss me. I told her, 'Not right now. My mom doesn't wanna be a grandmother before she's forty."

At least he listened to one *other* thing I'd said!

~ Chapter Eleven ~
Turkey Trouble

I don't know how it happened. Perhaps it was the pleading look in my husband John's eyes. Maybe it was because I'll do anything for a worthy cause. Whatever the reason, one Saturday morning, two weeks before Christmas, I stood in our kitchen, rubbing salt on breasts and shoving my hand up rear ends. I should mention we were cooking turkeys for a benefit. The proceeds would be used to supply shoes for local needy children.

Tranquility blanketed our home as John and I worked. Caught up in the mood, our children, Jonathan and Joseph, called a truce to their incessant bickering and played a game at the kitchen table. Norman Rockwell couldn't have painted a more perfect scene. It didn't last long.

"Pull the neck out of my bird, would ya. The cavity is too small for my hand."

Just over twelve years earlier, John and I had stood before God, our family and our friends, and started our married life together. My memory is sometimes sketchy, but I don't think the vow, "for better or worse," pertained to extracting necks out of turkey rumps.

I sighed and brushed a strand of hair away from my eyes, shuddering as cold, slimy poultry skin slid across my fingers. I hope he realizes how much I love him. This gal doesn't play turkey proctologist for just anyone.

The Toilet is Over-Flowing &
The Dog is Wearing My Underwear!
Debbie Roppolo

This should have been a simple task—reach in, grab the neck, mission complete. Easy, right? Not where I was concerned.

I'd been in unfortunate incidents before—falling into the Christmas tree, getting into the wrong car in a parking lot, and being knocked unconscious by a German shepherd. But now my pinkie ring wedged on something inside the bird, and that topped my list of mishaps.

My stomach churned as I imagined a trek to the ER, a rancid turkey wedged on my hand. No doubt, I'd see a PTA parent I knew. I'd be the topic of conversation at the next meeting. "We knew it was just a matter of time before Debbie's cheese slipped off the cracker," people would say. "And prancing into the emergency room, wearing Tom Turkey on her hand like it was the Crown Jewels proves it." *That will never happen—not if I can help it.* Sitting in a chair, I put my hand on the floor, my foot on the bird, and pulled. I tumbled backward and landed with a thump on the linoleum. The only thing I gained was a headache. Groaning, I propped myself up on one elbow and looked around.

John was busying himself with another bird. He smoothed a thin film of olive oil over the breast of his turkey. "There now. You'll bake nice and brown," he crooned.

I raised my eyebrow. Frankly, my husband's infatuation with his poultry was worrying me. "John... a little help over here. I've got—"

John turned, impatience blanketing his face as he took in the sight of me sitting spraddle-legged on the floor,

The Toilet is Over-Flowing &
The Dog is Wearing My Underwear!
Debbie Roppolo

the turkey between my knees. "Deb, please, there's no time for games."

Seriously? He thought I was sitting there, hobbled by a dead bird for fun? At that moment, his mustache could have had a horrible encounter with Nair™ hair remover, and no jury in the land would have convicted me.

"Does this," I asked, pointing at my hand, "look like I'm goofing off?"

John's eyes widened, then he shrugged. "Simple," he said finally. "Let go of the neck and pull your hand out."

I hated his coolness. And I wasn't twelve. I wanted him, for once, to be just as emotional as I was. "Don't you think I would if I could?" I demanded, teetering on the verge of hysterics.

"Maybe you could cut it off," Jonathan suggested from his spot at the table.

Joseph looked up from his game, face tight with worry. "You're gonna cut Mommy's hand off?"

"Not the hand, dummy, the turkey," Jonathan retorted.

"Oh, I thought I'd take it to show-and-tell if she didn't need it," Joseph mumbled, obviously disappointed over the loss of such a great (but gory) show-and-tell item.

"No one is gonna cut off anything," John grumbled. Holding the turkey under his arm like a football, he gave it a yank. It didn't budge. "There's gotta be some way to get this off," he said, ignoring the I-told-you-so look I gave him, and leading me to the sink.

My mind rode on an emotional roller coaster as I imagined my life WTIT (With Turkey In Tow). I wouldn't be able to hug my children for fear of knocking them unconscious. And what about dancing with John? There's

46

The Toilet is Over-Flowing &
The Dog is Wearing My Underwear!
Debbie Roppolo

nothing more unromantic than slow-dancing with poultry slung over my husband's shoulder.

But on a positive note, I'd no longer supervise Joseph's outdoor play dates. No one would entrust their children to a person who always had a pack of yapping, hungry dogs in tow.

John gave the turkey another tug. "This isn't coming off," he sighed. "I don't know what we're gonna do. But look at the bright side. You could be a poster girl for

Butterball™."

I gritted my teeth and fought the urge to bop him in the nose with my bird. Comedian.

"But I might have a solution." John took the cap off the bottle of olive oil. "Put your hand over the sink."

The phone rang as John poured oil into the turkey. Hope bubbled inside me as I felt my hand move more freely.

"Phone," Jonathan mumbled, not taking his eyes off the board game.

"We're a little busy right now," John said. "You get it."

"What do I say?"

"Anything. You'll think of something," his father replied.

There are certain things you shouldn't tell a teen. That they can use your debit card, vehicle, or say "anything" they want.

Keeping a wary eye on Joseph (who he suspected of cheating) Jonathan frowned and answered the phone on the sixth ring. "Hello? Yeah... they're both here, but they're busy."

The Toilet is Over-Flowing &
The Dog is Wearing My Underwear!
Debbie Roppolo

"Hope this works," John said, giving the bird a jerk. There was a suctioning sound, like a cow pulling her hoof out of mud, and then my hand was free.

John wiped his hands on a dishtowel. "I'll take the call now."

Jonathan frowned and motioned his father away. "Look, if you must know," he told the caller. "My dad asked Mama to pull a turkey neck out of his butt. Now her hand is stuck. See why they're busy? Oh no, thank you," he said with false politeness.

Jonathan smirked as he hung up. "Phone solicitor. I don't think they'll call here again."

And they haven't.

~ Chapter Twelve ~
Klutzin' Around the
Christmas Tree

In many cultures, Christmas is a cherished holiday. It's the one time of the year that peace, goodwill, and charity prospers, except in my house. Five minutes after they open the last gift, the year's hottest-selling toys are tossed aside like fruitcakes. My two children fight over who'll strap the cat to a model rocket, while the dog vomits stolen candy canes into my slipper. It's enough to make anyone empathize with Scrooge.

One year, I announced I would decorate the Christmas tree, alone. It was for the best, really. My preschooler, Joseph's idea of stringing garland is tying an end to the dog and letting it run around the trunk, wrapping up anyone in the way. My older son, Jonathan, leaps off the ladder, trying to slam-dunk the angel on the tree's top. In the end, the finished product resembles a wedge of moldy Swiss cheese, and I have the urge to hijack a Hershey's™ chocolate truck and eat its inventory.

"I don't think it's a good idea," my husband, John, objected. "Decorating a tree takes time and a bit of coordination. You lack both."

He had a point. I'm the only person I know who was knocked unconscious by a dog, made a high school acting performance a contact sport, and rode a scooter off the front porch, breaking my wrist. The previous Christmas, I slipped on ice and plowed into a group of carolers in our driveway, knocking them over like bowling pins.

The Toilet is Over-Flowing &
The Dog is Wearing My Underwear!
Debbie Roppolo

Still, anyone could shove a big stick into a metal stand and push fake limbs into place. I frowned and leaned closer to my husband. "Just what are you trying to say?" John fidgeted and cleared his throat. "Nothing really," he mumbled. "You're just... just..."

"Just a klutz," Jonathan interjected.

Joseph looked up from the picture he was coloring.

"Mama isn't cuts. If she were cuts, she would be bleeding."

"Not 'cuts', you dork. *Klutz*, meaning she's very clumsy," Jonathan informed his brother.

This, coming from a person who, the day before, slipped on a Tic Tac™ and fell face-first into a bladder pad display at the grocery store.

I waited until the family was asleep before lugging the Christmas boxes from the attic. I envisioned their joy when they awakened to a classic holiday atmosphere—fire crackling in the fireplace, baked cookies perfuming the air, and twinkling lights illuminating the living room. All completed by me, the klutz.

Four hours and a scratched hand later (I'd mistaken my cat's ear for a Christmas ornament) my living room resembled a crime scene. Boxes occupied the sofa, beaded garland hung from the ceiling fan, and only the lower half of the eight-foot tree was decorated.

"It's for my family, gotta get it done," I chanted, ignoring the searing pain in my calves as I stretched to hang a glittered snowflake.

"The same people who allow you to butt-dip because they leave the toilet seat up at night," my inner voice pointed out.

The Toilet is Over-Flowing &
The Dog is Wearing My Underwear!
Debbie Roppolo

Still, it was the holiday season, and my brood would have the childish wonder and joy a decorated tree brings.

The only thing unfinished was the top.

I learned, as I balanced on the arm of the loveseat, gravity wasn't my friend, and people, unlike cartoon characters, don't float through the atmosphere, light as paper. I grabbed air as I tumbled headfirst into the tree. Ornaments fell like raindrops, and pine needles scratched my face on my trip to the floor.

As the massive bush swayed, I could imagine the headlines the next morning: TREE RELIATES FOR BAD DECORATING. KNOCKS SURBURBAN MOM UNCONSCIOUS. INDIFFERENT FAMILY DEMANDS BREAKFAST.

I sighed in relief as the stand settled on its bottom. I've never been very talkative at social gatherings, but plastic pine needles impaled in my eyebrows wasn't the conversation starter I wanted.

"What's with all the noise?" Jonathan demanded, walking into the room. He stared at the ornaments around my prostrate form. "What are you doing?"

"Making carpet angels," I snapped. I pulled a plastic berry out of my ear and continued, "If you must know, I fell into the tree." There, I said it. Steeling myself, I waited to hear laughter, a barrage of *"I told you, you're a klutz."*

Instead, he grabbed my hand and clutched it to his chest. "Please tell me nothing is broken."

A lump formed in my throat. I was fortunate to have a child so concerned about my well-being. Jonathan's compassion showed the genuine spirit of Christmas.

"I'm fine, just a tad beat up," I replied, managing a watery smile.

The Toilet is Over-Flowing &
The Dog is Wearing My Underwear!
Debbie Roppolo

Avoiding my gaze, Jonathan muttered, "Umm, that's great, but I was talking about the ornaments."

The Toilet is Over-Flowing &
The Dog is Wearing My Underwear!
Debbie Roppolo

~ Chapter Thirteen~
One French Fry Short

There's a hush about the house that makes me uneasy, incapable of concentrating on the task at hand. Oh sure, some say "Silence is golden," but in my house, that's never a good thing. It means either my teenaged son, Jonathan, is shorting out the house phone by drooling over a female conversationalist, or my five-year-old, Joseph, is playing connect-the-dots on the Dalmatian with a permanent marker.

I can't say I don't enjoy being a mom. Often, there are moments that'd make a Hallmark™ card writer cry— spring flowers plucked by grimy hands and presented in a soda can, "I love you, Mommy" pictures created in crayon and taped to the fridge, and half-eaten cookies brought home from school to share.

But I realize my boys are on a mission to make the cheese slip off my cracker.

Dirty clothes, strong enough to take over humanity, litter the floor of my teen's room. Fuzzy, lumpy creatures, once peanut butter sandwiches, establish colonies under his bed. One day, I left my dental records with my husband, took a deep breath, and entered the den of chaos. Jonathan eyed me coolly from his perch of blankets piled high on his bed.

"Don't you think you should tidy up in here, at least forge a trail to your door?" I demanded. "Just now a dust bunny tapped on my shoe and begged me to end its suffering."

53

The Toilet is Over-Flowing &
The Dog is Wearing My Underwear!
Debbie Roppolo

My son made a sweeping glance and then turned a page in his book. "Looks fine to me."

"But what if company comes over?"

"Just shut the door to my room." He shrugged. "Don't see why you're getting flustered over a little mess."

I sucked in my cheeks. "Honey, I've seen demolition areas more organized. Don't forget, just the other day our pregnant cat got lost under your bed."

"Found her before she had kittens," he snapped.

"Besides, cleaning is your job."

My "job" was harsh enough to make the toughest war monger beg for mercy. I've scraped booger self-portraits off car windows, rescued cell phones from toilets, scooped corn flakes out of the fishbowl, sometimes all before breakfast. There are streaking sessions in the backyard at bath time and games of hide-n-seek in lingerie racks at department stores. I've pulled lemon seeds from ears and explained why cats couldn't be dyed like Easter eggs. Believing we should leave no family secrets untold, Joseph once told dinner guests the doctor gave me hemorrhoids for bronchitis. Not to let his brother have all the attention, Jonathan chimed in, saying his father had a pap smear (he meant CPAP) machine for sleep apnea.

When I was a child, my mother had conversations with wet towels, asked about the condition of my underwear in front of friends, and boogied in the driveway when the school year began. At the time, I thought she was one French fry short of a Happy Meal™. Now, as I rescue my underwear off the family dog, I'm understanding the reason for her madness.

~ Chapter Fourteen ~
Adventures at the Optometrist's

"What time is it?" my teenager, Jonathan, grumbled.

"I can't believe you made me come along. I don't wanna be here." He pointed at his four-year-old brother, prostrate on the floor. "And I think you've finally bored Joseph to death."

I sighed and flipped through a magazine. You would've thought I asked him to scrub toilets at the gas station.

But I really couldn't blame him. The wait for the optometrist is atrocious. During one appointment, I'm convinced I saw an infant walk, graduate college, and get married, all in one visit. Not to mention the last time I came, I sat next to a guy who insisted on showing me a cyst under his arm, which he claimed looked like Benjamin Franklin. I don't relish the exam, either. The room is the size of my bedroom closet. People invading my personal space irritate me, and the doctor always sits knee-to-knee. It's just my opinion, but unless he's placing a wedding ring on my finger, there's no reason to be that close. Even if, how would I explain it to my husband, John? "Hi honey, they gave me a free spouse with the purchase of contact lenses."

Therefore, for the past several months, I played cat-and-mouse with the eye doctor. I ignored post cards that went from happy faces to pointing fingers. I was "not

The Toilet is Over-Flowing &
The Dog is Wearing My Underwear!
Debbie Roppolo

home" when his office called to schedule an appointment. But when I kissed our porch post goodbye and tried to wrap Christmas lights around John, I knew I couldn't avoid it any longer. I needed an eye exam.

This time, the waiting room was almost empty. "That's good. You can relax while you wait," my husband said when he dropped the boys and me off. He had to be kidding.

And in the few minutes we'd been in the waiting room, I'd rescued pen tops from my four-year old's nose, played hide-n-seek with my cell phone among the couch cushions, and grabbed my purse off the back of an older woman's wheelchair (for a few tense moments she thought I was mugging her) where Joseph had hanged it. The word "relax" wasn't in my vocabulary.

I wished, as I plucked my youngest off the back of a chair, businesses would develop a service where children were checked in like coats, leaving the parent to sit in the lobby in peace. I imagined my kids sitting on a shelf, numbered tags dangling off their ears.

"Don't know why you're giggling," Jonathan grumbled. He kicked at a pattern in the carpet. "This is the most boring place on earth."

"That's not true. You can find excitement anywhere, even at the optometrist. Just depends on how you look at things," I remarked. "For example, that lady in the wheelchair slapped me in the head with her purse, rolled over my foot, and threatened to have me arrested. Can't find that kind of excitement at an arcade," I pointed out.

The Toilet is Over-Flowing &
The Dog is Wearing My Underwear!
Debbie Roppolo

Just I was just considering strapping glass cola bottles to my eyes and forgoing the exam, a nurse, the living version of Barbie, called my name.

My stomach lurched as I walked into an exam room.

There, a few inches from the door, lay an eye on the floor.

"There it is," Wannabe Barbie chirped, picking up the eye.

"The doctor dropped a head earlier, and this popped out."

Jonathan gagged as she blew on the object and wiped it on her shirt.

"We all looked, even the patient, Mister Sambs. But he couldn't see anything."

"I'm sure he couldn't," I mumbled. I licked my lips and wiped the sweat off my forehead. "Tell me, does the doctor always get that rough?"

Wannabe Barbie stared at me, then laughed. "Oh no, the head was a model. Dr. Ables was trying to show the patient how a certain eye disease progressed. You're hilarious," she said, walking out of the room.

I wasn't sure about my hilarity. But I was right. You can find excitement anywhere, even at the optometrist's.

The Toilet is Over-Flowing &
The Dog is Wearing My Underwear!
Debbie Roppolo

~ Chapter Fifteen ~
Age is a State of Mind— Too Bad I Can't Find Mine

I never gave aging a single thought. Raised with the philosophy of "Pretty is as pretty does," I'd learned to look past people's physical appearances and see beauty within the soul. I didn't consider getting older until my fortieth birthday.

Nothing appeared out of the ordinary until I bought wine and offered the cashier my driver's license.

"You're joking, right?" she asked.

I frowned and shook my head.

The cashier chewed her lip, giggling. "Oh, I get it. I'm on a hidden camera show." She leaned over, smiled and waved at my purse. "Ya got me! By the way, Mom, see you during school break and hope Dad's constipation is better."

I jerked my bag away. "You're not on camera," I huffed. "I presented my ID because it's the law. You have to be at least twenty-one to buy alcohol."

The girl reddened, then took a deep breath. "Aren't you cute," she cooed. Handing me my change, she called for a carry-out.

"I can carry my own Twinkies™ and wine," I protested.

"Nonsense, it's a service we offer our old, ah, I mean, valued customers."

The Toilet is Over-Flowing &
The Dog is Wearing My Underwear!
Debbie Roppolo

The following day, I received correspondence from
AARP, and a flier for a senior living center. "I don't get it,"
I complained, thumping the mail on the kitchen table.
"Today a guy almost shoved me into traffic to make way for
a pretty woman, and later, a boy scout tried walking me
across the street so I 'wouldn't break a hip.'"

My teenager, Jonathan, took a bite of his sandwich,
eyeing me coolly. "Simple," he said, licking the mayo off
his fingers. "You're old."

"Real old," the youngest, Joseph, chimed in.

I sucked in my cheeks. "Anything else I can get you?
Perhaps some chips before I turn into dust and get sucked
into the air conditioner vents?"

"You're not that old," Jonathan said, rolling his
eyes.

Yep, you look a little better than my first-grade
teacher," Joseph chirped.

How old is she?"

"Sixty."

Somehow, that didn't make me feel better.

I looked in the hallway mirror, shocked when my
mother's image stared back. I squinted and leaned in
closer. My pulse quickened as I realized my mama might
look better. She had a smooth, peaches-and-cream
complexion. I had enough freckles and age spots to
make our Dalmatian jealous. Laugh lines surrounded the
corners of my mouth and eyes—I don't remember
laughing that much—and I swore the beginnings of a
female mustache covered my top lip.

The Toilet is Over-Flowing &
The Dog is Wearing My Underwear!
Debbie Roppolo

Later, when my husband, John, arrived home from work, I grabbed him by the suit lapels and demanded, "Who do you find more attractive, Mama or me?"

He stared at me, incredulous. "You must be nuts," he said, loosening my grasp.

"Are you trying out for the Jerry Springer show? You, of course. Sicko."

Convinced my husband was placating me, I began forming a plan. Unless he wanted to be wed to a female version of Doc Holliday, I had to hobble the aging process.

I wasn't, however, prepared to mortgage my house to regain my youthful look. Instead, I'd go the cheap, er, *green* route, and give myself an organic makeover, beginning with my hair.

I remembered reading somewhere that the ancient Romans fought gray hair by making a paste of chopped earthworms and mud and rubbing it on their heads.

The next day I ventured out to the local bait shop and purchased a tub of wigglers and dirt. "There's a nice little shady spot out on Sleepin' Bear Lake," the elderly cashier said. "Bunch of people been catching bass there."

"Oh, this isn't for fishing, I'm gonna rub the worms on my head."

The older man raised an eyebrow. "What's that? Gonna put 'em in your hair then stick your head under the water? Well, if that don't beat all. Might catch on, though. I..."

"That's not what it's for," I interrupted, blushing and scratching at the price sticker on the container.

"What the devil is it for?"

"I'm gonna make a paste out of worms and rub it through my hair."

The Toilet is Over-Flowing &
The Dog is Wearing My Underwear!
Debbie Roppolo

"If that isn't the gul-darndest thing I ever heard." The cashier sighed, shook his head, and then spat a stream of tobacco juice into a nearby spittoon. "I swanny, I'll never figure you young people and your fancy new ideas out."

At that moment, I couldn't have been happier.

The Toilet is Over-Flowing &
The Dog is Wearing My Underwear!
Debbie Roppolo

~ Chapter Sixteen ~
Honey, Where's the Instruction Booklet on This Kid?

In this age when ovens can receive and reply to text messages, society doesn't want for knowledge, though sometimes we need to exercise it more. A few seconds on the computer, tablet, or cell phone and we're zipping down the information highway gathering facts like Pacman™ after frightened ghosts. But shortly after the last dinosaur roamed the earth and before the cell phone (my generation), people quenched their thirst for knowledge through experiences, advice from elders, or by reading it in a book or instruction manual.

A few months after marriage, I became pregnant but didn't obsess like some other young women. I didn't bronze the pregnancy test or save it for the baby book; nor did I pick out curtains for the nursery the first time my face and the toilet bowl became acquainted. I'd grown up on a ranch and bore witness to cows and horses giving birth—they made it seem simple. And besides, there were hundreds of books on the subject, and any of them could answer questions I might have. Wrong.

During the fifth month of pregnancy, I found none of them could explain why my ankles seemed to have traded places with my knees, and why, on a good day, roadkill could have won a beauty contest against me. And nothing explained that labor hurt worse than an impacted tooth. *Raising the baby will be simpler*, I always thought. Again, I was wrong. Teaching our dog to tap-dance would have been

The Toilet is Over-Flowing &
The Dog is Wearing My Underwear!
Debbie Roppolo

easier. Nothing I read explained why Jonathan withheld his spit-up until I was wearing white or resisted loudly passing gas until we were in public and a large crowd was present. No one believes the baby did it. But all that paled in comparison to one morning when Jonathan was six months old.

Beads of perspiration formed on my forehead as I watched Jonathan thrash and scream in his crib. My most recent parenting book had assured me that taking a quick trip in the car was a great way to calm a fussy baby. That option was out. I'd already driven around the block so many times I was convinced my neighbors thought I couldn't find my way home, or I was practicing being a NASCAR driver.

No, it was time to call in the experts. I took a deep breath, and swallowing my pride, I called the biggest authority I knew about child-raising...my mother. Regardless of age or gender, just the thought of reaching out to one's mother in times of need is a comfort. I turned into a sobbing mass of gelatin the minute I heard Mama's voice. Between gasps, I explained either Jonathan was ill, or he was forming a plan to take control of the family by driving me insane. And based on the fact he'd kept me sleep-deprived for the past six months, I was leaning towards the latter.

"Don't be a goose," Mama admonished. "How old is he now? Have you started him on solids? If that's the case, he's constipated."

"I-I have," I stuttered. "That must be it. What can I do?" I twisted the phone cord around my finger, hoping the solution wasn't my mother's cure-all for everything...a

The Toilet is Over-Flowing &
The Dog is Wearing My Underwear!
Debbie Roppolo

soapy enema. If I must, I must, but I didn't relish the thought of my shirt being painted with my child's bowel movement.

"Simple. Prune juice."

I made a face. That was something they gave elderly people when they were in the rest home, and for me during some points in my pregnancy, but not babies. "Are you sure?"

Mama's voice took on that listen-up-or-you're-in-trouble tone. "Yep, a tad of that will get the plumbing flowing again," she assured me. "Just dilute it so..."   I didn't bother to listen to the rest. Mama prattled on a great deal about many things, and I didn't have time for a lecture today.

As luck would have it, I had a bottle of the juice hidden in the recesses of my pantry, visible to only dust bunnies and the occasional visiting house spider.
I handed Jonathan eight ounces of straight prune juice in his bottle. "Drink up, Buttercup."

It impressed me that he drank the stuff without a whimper. Another eight ounces will really do the trick. I gave the baby another serving.

One lesson that I learned as a new mom was to seize a chance for fun when I could. It overjoyed me when my husband, John, took Jonathan and me out for an early supper that night.

Every woman, at some time in her life, has the fantasy of people staring when she enters a room. It perplexed me when we walked into our favorite Mexican restaurant and caught the stare of a gentleman near the door. A look of complete revulsion blanketed his face as I walked past, carrying Jonathan. I knew my lack of sleep

The Toilet is Over-Flowing &
The Dog is Wearing My Underwear!
Debbie Roppolo

left me with bags big enough to check in at the airport, but I didn't think I looked that bad.

His wife was the opposite, offering me a smile. "How can you act like that's normal? It's disgusting," the man said.

Anger turned to confusion as I saw the woman pat her husband's arm and say, "Don't worry about it, dear. She probably doesn't realize it yet."

I slid into a nearby booth. *Realize what?* I didn't have to speculate for long. A thick layer of disgusting smelling, salsa verde colored goop covered my arm and the front of my shirt. An equally large trail of slime stretched up Jonathan's back, beginning at the diaper, ending at his neckline—it was his bowel movement.

"John," I hissed. "We have to leave. We have to leave now!" I flipped Jonathan around and showed John the mess.

For once, I didn't have to repeat myself. "Let's get out of here," John croaked.

My stomach churned like a washing machine. In my lifetime I'd cleaned many a stall on Daddy's ranch, and in six months, changed enough diapers to fill a dumpster, but to have it plastered on my body, that was different. I held Jonathan at arm's length as we raced through the restaurant. Everyone who didn't see our entrance had the pleasure of seeing Jonathan's back as we made our hasty retreat.

At the door, we bumped into a young couple that gazed dumbstruck at our son. Flashing the couple a winning smile, John said, "Whatever you do, don't eat the green chicken enchiladas!"

The Toilet is Over-Flowing &
The Dog is Wearing My Underwear!
Debbie Roppolo

~ Chapter Seventeen ~
All Because of a Bra

I couldn't deny the truth. For the past month I'd pleaded that it hang on, assuring it a well-deserved rest. We'd had so many adventures together, taking walks through the hills, and an occasional run on a hotel treadmill. But as I stared at the black mass laying on the floor one morning, I knew after many months of service, the end had come—the elastic in my sports bra died.

Just the thought of walking into a department store made my stomach churn. The air always makes my eyes feel like packing peanuts, even when I wear glasses. The lack of moisture glue my lips together—the combined result makes me resemble an over-sized seahorse. And inevitably, I'll see someone I know. The last time I took a shopping trip, I bumped into a neighbor. Two hours later, I arrived home and found a care basket, complete with a "get well soon" card, sitting on my doorstep.

As much as I hated shopping, this trip was even more dreaded. I'd have to take my (then) three-year-old son, Joseph, with me. Shopping with a young child is challenging. They tire easily, and their whining would make even a Stepford wife lose control. But taking Joseph would be even more trying. Besides the usual toddler antics, he was diagnosed with autism just a few months earlier. During the weeks after the diagnosis, I realized that my son's disability wasn't my fault, and there wasn't anything I could have done to prevent it. But I hated venturing into public. I wanted everyone to see Joseph for the precious

The Toilet is Over-Flowing &
The Dog is Wearing My Underwear!
Debbie Roppolo

child he was and not his autism. And every stare or snicker when he flapped his hands or showed echolalia (repetitive use of words or phrases) ripped my heart a little more. On this venture, I was relieved to see that the Target™ parking lot was almost deserted. It was before noon and the college students choosing to stay in town during spring break had yet to slink out of bed.

During previous shopping trips, I've observed the bravest looking of men break into a cold sweat and take detours around the women's undergarment section. My older son has done wild buck impersonations, flattening mannequins in his haste to escape the sight of bras and panties.

Joseph, in the past, has been content to use my best bra as a beanie for the cat's head, with company present. So, I thought there'd be no issues with my grabbing what I needed during this shopping trip. I was wrong. Joseph became more agitated, rocking faster the closer I pushed him and the cart to the lingerie section.

During previous trips, my son discovered how his squeals and screams bounced off the wall of the store. Now he used this to his advantage. He waited until I was absorbed in my "perfect bra quest" before yelling, in his best commercial announcer's voice, "Oh no, this is all wrong. You need the Genie Bra. It lifts and separates..."

Startled, I grabbed the cart to keep from tumbling sideways into a pantyhose display. *Oh, please let me be the only one who heard that.* My face reddened as a shopper strode by, one brow raised in consternation. For a moment, I wished to turn into a chameleon and blend in with the

The Toilet is Over-Flowing &
The Dog is Wearing My Underwear!
Debbie Roppolo

girdles.   "Joseph, we don't say things like that..."
"It comes in three exciting colors!"
As he went through the entire commercial, I realized the hilarity of it. At that moment, I realized that life was too short to care what people thought of me or Joseph. I leaned across the bar of the cart, enjoying the first laughter I'd had in months, gifted to me by the innocence of my child, and all because of a bra.

~ Chapter Eighteen ~
You Just Gotta Wear Shades

I thought I was, for once, prepared. Armed with enough women's magazines to supply a library for a year, I poured through every article about fitness I could find. I lunged when I reached for veggies out of the fridge and squatted to the point my family thought I had toileting issues. Yes, I'd have that beach body every 40-something woman craved. Too bad I started toning a week before our vacation to the coast.

Sometimes in everyone's existence when Life slaps them in the back of the head and yells, "What were you thinking?" I got my wake-up call when I stood before a full-length mirror, clad in a peach-colored one-piece swimsuit at my friend, Calli's, house.

"You look pretty good," she complimented me. It was obvious she'd either put friendship above honesty, or she'd gone temporarily blind. Calli wasn't seeing the same reflection I was. Cellulite decorated my upper thighs like lumps of rancid cottage cheese, and my butt hung like a couple of flat beanbags.

I struggled to pull the Lycra over my thighs, wincing as it snapped my skin. The peach-colored suit made me look and feel like the grandmother of an Oscar Meyer™ wiener. "You've got to be kidding."

The Toilet is Over-Flowing &
The Dog is Wearing My Underwear!
Debbie Roppolo

Calli cleared her throat and walked around, studying me at every angle. "Well... you could wear shorts, and perhaps a short-sleeved shirt..."

"And maybe ankle-length pants, and a bag over my head with the words 'PG-14 rating alarming image' written across the front?" I grumbled.

My friend and I agreed that with time (and help from Calli's fashion sense) cute beach outfits could be arranged. Calli sighed and shook her head. "But those legs," she began.

I frowned and crossed my arms. "What about them?"

She pointed at my tanned arms. "Your upper body looks like it belongs to another person. I almost need sunglasses to look at those white legs."

With her help, I applied self-tanner to my legs. Three hours later, I looked like an Oompa-Loompa. "There's always tanning beds," Calli suggested. I dismissed that idea, partly because of the ultraviolet rays, but largely because of the fear of being forgotten. I'd once seen a forgotten chicken breast on a George Foreman™ grill. The look wasn't attractive, and certainly not on me.

During the rest of the week, I researched the Internet for ways to darken the skin on my legs. Finally, the morning before the trip, I saw the solution—coffee grounds mixed with olive oil. And my husband and I had just finished our morning java.

My heart sang and I almost danced my way to the bathroom. Humming, I smeared on the mixture, imagining the tropical tan I'd have, making me the envy of the beach. I was just smearing on the last bit when the door flung open. There stood my twelve-year-old son, mouth agape as he took in the sight of his mother, clad in her nightshirt and

The Toilet is Over-Flowing &
The Dog is Wearing My Underwear!
Debbie Roppolo

covered in coffee grounds. Silence blanketed the room as we regarded one another. I broke the spell by clearing my throat. "Umm.... Mama got really excited over coffee this morning."

Joseph blinked, then shook his head. "Wash your legs, please. You smell like a Starbucks™."

At that point, I was considering handing out free sunglasses at the beach, courtesy of my blinding-white legs.

~ Chapter Nineteen ~
Clark has Nothing on Me

I'll admit it. Jealousy is my companion when friends embark on vacations. With smiles that rival beauty pageant contestants, my girlfriends and their families pile into perfectly packed vehicles, leaving pasty faced only to return Coppertone™ spokespeople. I endure days (okay, an hour, max) of DVDs showcasing their Brady Bunch type adventures where the only mishap was leaving the cap off the toothpaste.

The vacation gods don't smile on my family—in fact, we're like the Clark Griswold family from the *National Lampoon*™ movies. My children do their part to ensure the latter. There has been hide-n-seek with the pet mouse among the suitcases, spit wad art decorating the car windows, and several choruses of "I'm bored," all before we leave the driveway.

In the past, we've lost our older son in the elevator of a hotel and pulled him off a plane bound for Cancun (our destination was Missouri). I've learned through the years of family trips that the smell of boys' feet and day-old spilled ice cream embedded in upholstery is indistinguishable, and the funk of both have the power to render the other car passengers speechless.

Admittedly, I've done my part in adding to the mayhem. Blessed with all the skills of a drunken navigator, I've read maps upside-down, and miss-programmed the GPS, resulting in a detour through a farmer's cornfield,

The Toilet is Over-Flowing &
The Dog is Wearing My Underwear!
Debbie Roppolo

courtesy of a narrow gravel farm road, and I've humored hotel employees with suction-cup animal impersonations by running face-first into clear glass hotel doors. Once, I provided "the biggest thrill in a while" (according to the man- ager) when I flashed an entire rural restaurant because my dress was unintentionally tucked into the back of my dress.

After the dress episode, my dear hubby, John, decided that we might take a break from our adventures. "A year off will allow us to regenerate our financial resources," he claimed.

"Regenerate resources" my tater tots. This, coming from a guy who breaks into a sweat at the mention of us all taking just a trip to the grocery store. The truth is, he's scared of his face appearing on the side of a milk carton or on the news—a victim of our misadventures.

I made it my mission to prove we could have an uneventful, normal vacation. For the next year, I clipped coupons and cut back on unnecessary expenses, except for coffee. Mr. Coffee™ and I have been in a steady relationship since college, without him I couldn't remember my name, and I was unwilling to end the affair for anyone—even my family.

Finally, with money in hand, I pleaded my case to John. "You've been working too hard; we never see you. Plus," I reasoned, "everything that could possibly happen has."

He sighed and stared at the ceiling. "Well, we haven't been hit by a meteor or run over by a herd of bison. But plan a trip. I'm a glutton for punishment." The night before the trip, I packed the car with

73

The Toilet is Over-Flowing &
The Dog is Wearing My Underwear!
Debbie Roppolo

organizational skills Martha Stewart would be envious of. I played a marathon of *Leave it to Beaver*™ episodes for my boys and ensured their good behavior by bribing them with promises of trips to Chuck E. Cheese™.

Everything went as planned the next day. The boys, with visions of pepperonis dancing in their heads, read and quietly looked out the car windows. Convinced our streak of bad vacations were over, I convinced John to stop at a gift shop in a small town, an hour into the trip. Oblivious to my family's whereabouts, I browsed aisles of books that stimulated the imagination, and regal-looking figurines that begged the heart to buy them.

Finally, I emerged from the store and watched as my family drove away in our SUV. Annoyance replaced shock. John and I always teased each other, and no doubt this was his way of letting me know I'd taken too long.

Aww well… can't give him the satisfaction of seeing me irritated. Might as well play along and give everyone a good laugh. Screaming like a woman possessed, I raced after the SUV, arms waving over my head. I wondered, as my sandals slipped over the pavement, why my husband was speeding up. Didn't he know when to stop a joke? As I ran, I heard a voice call out, "Ah… Mom, we're back here!"

At that same moment, the SUV stopped, and an elderly man stuck his balding head out the driver's window, confusion plastered across his wizened face. I was chasing the wrong car. In my haste to one up my husband, I had been chasing the wrong car.

Our record for misadventures grew. Clark W. Griswold has nothing on us.

~Chapter Twenty~
Life is Beautiful—
Even When It's a Roller Coaster

"Bless your heart, you're burdened," is usually the comment from strangers to me after my twelve-year-old son, Joseph, has a meltdown. In the past, I almost fell over myself in my haste to offer an embarrassed apology and scoot away from what seemed like a throng of people as quickly as possible.

Now an older and wiser me, with teeth gritted, smiles and explains Joseph's actions-he has autism, and something in his surroundings has overstimulated him, thus the meltdown. Like an infomercial host, I explain ASD-what it is, symptoms, and how things in our environment might affect someone with autism. Sometimes, that's followed by a sad look from the other person, and they mutter, "My, my...you didn't ask for that, did you?"

In those circumstances, I bite my lip to keep sarcastic, almost hysterical laughter at bay. The stranger meant well. She was offering compassion, something often lacking in our society. But no, I didn't ask for my child, my heart, to have a neurological disorder.

Having a child on the autism spectrum is comparable to a roller-coaster ride. There are the up moments. Like when your child says for the first time, "Mama, I love you," and you've waited seven years to hear it because he's been almost completely non-verbal. Or countless hours of

The Toilet is Over-Flowing &
The Dog is Wearing My Underwear!
Debbie Roppolo

teaching and tears (because there doesn't seem to be comprehension), trying to get him to kick versus dribble the soccer ball into the net. But at the state Special Olympic games, he kicks it in on the very first try.

Then there are the times when you're at a restaurant, and your child is having a screaming, kicking fit because the waiter cut the burger in half, and Junior never eats his burger cut in half (kids on the spectrum like routine). Every eye (it seems) is focused on your family, and you wish you could crawl into that darn sandwich and hide from the world.

But this has been a journey of learning for me. I have discovered how to look past physical appearances and abilities and see people's determination and beauty within. Though I'm a perpetual work in progress, I have been a scholar of lowering the walls, practicing empathy, moving past emotional scars, and loving with my whole heart.

And Joseph has become my biggest teacher. He has taught me to appreciate the smaller things in life: the majesty of the sun setting on the hills; the magic in a bird's song; delicious aromas of the earth as it awakens in the mornings. Nothing is to be taken for granted, especially the sweet, sing-song chant of a child's conversation.

One Saturday, Joseph walked into the living room and watched as I danced to "Uptown Funk." Wordlessly, he stepped in front of me and began stomping in time to the music–an accomplishment for someone on the Autism spectrum. Tears clouded my vision. I was grateful when the song ended because I have all the grace of an ostrich on ice and I wasn't prepared to spend Saturday morning in the emergency room.

The Toilet is Over-Flowing &
The Dog is Wearing My Underwear!
Debbie Roppolo

Joseph chewed his finger as he studied me. *"La vita e bella,* Mama?" he questioned, reading the front of my shirt.

"Yes, Joseph, *La vita e bella.* It means 'Life is beautiful.'"

And it is, even when it's a roller coaster ride of emotions.

First appeared in Mothers Always Write e-zine (07/2015).

www.ingramcontent.com/pod-product-compliance
Lightning Source LLC
Chambersburg PA
CBHW060534030426
42337CB00021B/4256